IN MEDITERRANEAN AIR

IN MEDITERRANEAN AIR

ANN STANFORD

THE VIKING PRESS

New York

First published in 1977 by The Viking Press
625 Madison Avenue, New York, N.Y. 10022
Published simultaneously in Canada by
The Macmillan Company of Canada Limited

Library of Congress Cataloging in Publication Data
Stanford. Ann.
In Mediterranean air.
I. Title.
PS3537.T1815147   811'.5'4   76-28179
ISBN 0-670-39587-0

Printed in the United States of America
Set in IBM Journal

Most of these poems originally appeared in
Atlantic Monthly, California Quarterly,
Chicago Tribune Magazine, Counter Measures,
Epos, The Literary Review, Marilyn, Michigan Quarterly,
The New Republic, The New Yorker, Poetry, Poetry Now,
Southern Review, Virginia Quarterly Review.

I wish to thank Evelyn Venable Mohr,
Lecturer in Classics at the
University of California, Los Angeles,
for her as always invaluable help
in the translation from Euripides. —A.S.

To Beth and Donald Straus

CONTENTS

ONE

Glimmerglass   3
Dreaming of Foxes   4
Strange   5
Once   6
I Thought Back and   7
Overlappings   8
The Wind Saying Winter   9
One April   10

TWO

Our Town   13
The Burning of Ilium   14
Libraries   16
Prophet   18
The Four Horsemen   19
Mr. D   21
Language   22
Heat Wave   23
Holding Our Own   24
The Artist Underground   26
On Music   28

THREE

The Women of Perseus
Danae   33
The Graeae   41
Medusa   42
Andromeda   44
Perseus   46

FOUR

After September 51
Love Song 52

Into the Bestiary
1 / The Owl Inside 53
2 / The Bird Lagoon 54
3 / The Fish Cage 55
4 / The Mole Ride 56

Despite All That 57
Watching the Break-Up 58
Driving Eastward 60
Down, Down 61
Unwinding the Glacier 62
In Summer 63

FIVE

In Mediterranean Air
At the Villa 67
The Pursuer 68
In the Garden 70
The Chase 71
On the Train 72
Incognito 73
Headquarters 74
Three 75
Outside 76
The Party 77
The Design 78

SIX

Exiles 83
Crossing 84
The Message 85
After Exile 86
The Turn 87
Listening to Color 88

ONE

GLIMMERGLASS

This lake is the center of the story.
All that happens the lake makes possible.
This lake has deeps for graves and shoals for building.

On a shoal in the lake there is a fortress
A house that resembles a ship, round which the tides
Drift in predictable fashion, like a cradle rocking.

All is at hand, lake trout rise to the hook
Deer come down to drink, easy for taking,
Ducks and geese by the bagful. Berries grow on the shore.

What a monotony of noble days and nights!
The cliffs softened by trees, the water birds calling
The lake glimmering as sun and stars take turns above it.

Outside the ring—the house, the lake, the shore—
The unbroken forest. There the enemy waits
Circling and stalking the house in the center.

Round within round to the very eye
That watches from the knothole, the heart that hides
In the house in the lake in the circle of the forest.

DREAMING OF FOXES

Dreaming of foxes
coyotes and the deer
that used to hang about the garden
nuzzling the fresh green
their breaths smelling of roses

I was tempted to wake
but saying, no, into
this dream I will dissolve
I will go
down into its well of water.

What will I find there
that the morning birds
will not carry away
those lakes of blue, teeming,
by snowy mountains.

Out of the mountains
came the birds in line
took the pieces of my dream
the shreds of lake water
threaded them among the trees
in the leaves where they sit waking.

STRANGE

and in what manner
morning comes
drifting across the skull
that lifts from sleep,
a boat rising on a wave
that slaps the harbor
the wall white with summer
where the cat licks its silver side
in the warm path
and says good morning
its pink mouth wide with sleep,
morning drifting down the leaves
broken as water falling
through the keen air
where once we rode
blithe in our woods.

ONCE

Off the road, a long drive through a wood
we came to a gate and gatehouses
by a courtyard. Circled, narrow
around a well and on
through the wood.

                     The house, a castle.
The turrets not for defense. Deserted
this palace. Nudging a lake
the terrace. Mist on the lake.
Swans lived there, but none in sight.

Surely from the reeds at the edge
a swan would come, half-rising out of water
its wide wings clapping, catching the air
and rising terrible over us, where we stood
a cold wind lacing the terrace
telling our bones this was deserted
not ours, and never could be.

I THOUGHT BACK AND

There I was
at the top of the walnut tree
in my old red sweater
my dress catching on twigs
my legs scratched from climbing.
Wind bent the boughs
almost to breaking:

　　Growing in every cell
　　I never once thought of you
　　thinking about me.

　　Your problem is forever looking
　　backward.
　　All you see is me
　　waiting for the next big
　　noisy gust of wind
　　to hang from.

　　All you see is me
　　not thinking of you,
　　old woman,
　　me singing.

OVERLAPPINGS

The trouble is we are always reminded of something
beside the point. *Games*, you say,
and appear the long ropes under the walnut tree
the swingboard knotted on the thick white rope;
we climb the fence, scrape our knees on the stucco
come home hungry, dirt-ringed from hiking.

Other summers. The bluebirds by the back door
decades ago. Now linnets trying to break in,
the dove, neck broken, against our window.
They overlap, shades in water
down under the surfaces of the spring
so clear and deep we drank from one summer.

Now one is dying and the other dead, the patriarchs
thin and tall, which world they live in
all these lives so shuffled together
these same scenes over and over, deeper and deeper repeated
their watery scarves stream round us, kill
that old child's morning game of resurrection.

THE WIND SAYING WINTER

Suppose I say to the wind
beating down from the north,
cold, knocking gravel from the roof
pelting me with the last walnuts—

Suppose I say *Stop*
putting my force against the wind
we have had enough.
All my mind goes out to the wind:

Stop bending the trees
making the eucalyptus leaves tangle
round skimpy limbs.
Hwew, the wind answers, *hwew, hwew.*

I give up on the wind.
It has come a long way
from some high, snow-covered desert.
But my own self I can talk to.

Stop, I say to my self.
Remember how things used to be.
Remember how you ran in the orchard,
up early?

The wind is still rising.
Limbs beat against the eaves.
Dust colors the air.

ONE APRIL

When I go away, this will become a picture
the big river flowing deep and still past the front door
the poinciana about to burst with red flowers
a few mosquitoes buzzing, but not yet many,
and the air heavy by the palmetto thicket.

Things are going to stay this way for a long time.
Whatever I do, my uncle is going to be here
smoking his cigarette, talking of shorthorn cattle
and Doll, the gardener, with his shears
will be snipping a mound of foliage early in the morning
while Esther stirs in the kitchen among pancakes.

I am leaving now, but the scene will never change.
If I come back, things will start again.

TWO

OUR TOWN

This is the village where we grew
Our fathers and their sires in line
The trees they planted shade the view
And the white houses shine.

The families here had come to stay
The preacher was the parson's son
And if one brother moved away
We kept the solid one.

We tended order in the town
Our lawns were trim, our hedges green
And in the countryside around
The furrows straight and clean.

We went to church, obeyed the laws
And voted on election day.
The peaceful farms surrounded us
The battles always far away.

And when the soldiers came to town
With drums and our flag overhead,
We watched them from the commons lawn
Until they shot us dead.

THE BURNING OF ILIUM

From *The Trojan Women* by Euripides

Throw in the torches!
Hold back the fire no longer!

I go forth from my country, my city struck with flames.
Get up, old foot, and carry me along
that I may hail once more my suffering city.
Great Troy, whose very sound breathed Asia once
your glorious name will soon be torn away.
You burn; already they are leading us as slaves
out of our earth. O gods! But why do I cry to the gods?
When I called on them before, they did not hear.

Ilium shines.
Fire burns in the chambers of the citadel
and in the city and on the highest parts of the walls.

Like smoke that fades on heaven's wing,
gashed by the spear, our country perishes.
Our roofbeams glow, wasted by blazing fire
and the devouring points of lances.

You, you that I bore, hear your mother's voice.
Old woman, wail. It is the dead you call.

I set my old limbs on the ground
and loudly beat the earth with both my hands.
I cry to the dead below. Unlucky husband!

O husband, husband, lost, unburied, without a friend,
you cannot know my doom,
dark there in the dark, death has covered the eyes
of the holy that the unholy have slain.

House of the gods, beloved city,
you feel the sharp-edged flame, the murdering spear
you will merge with the dear earth, without a name.

> The great wing of smoke darkens the sky
> the houses fall away from my sight
> the name will be gone from the land
> all are scattered and gone.

> Hear now, the citadel crashes!
> The quaking shakes the earth
> shatters the city.
> Troy is no longer.

Trembling legs, carry me on to the new life of bondage.
O wretched city! Earth that nourished my children!
I go down to the Achaean ships.

> . . .

> *And still out of the flames streaming the refugees*
> *under the smoke's black wing, the shadows,*
> *the dust of cities falling, scattered, unburied,*
> *the mother holding the dead child, the fire-ripped*
> *clothes, the temples broken, the gods stone-eyed*
> *above cold offerings, the bells scattered,*
> *the roofbeams fallen, lost, separate,*
> *moving somewhere under the wine-dark sun.*

LIBRARIES

Always being burned by vandals
of whatever name
next to the temple
papyri
browned, curled, the paint flaked off
the secrets of the gods
a black smoke only.

Or breaking through the ill-kept door—
the scriptorium littered with fallen flowers
the acanthus scattered among vowels
the blossoms not of this world, the enameled petals
gilt stems falling underfoot, saints
and the pointed hills crowding the margins,
the prayers divided, the visions gobbed in blood
the girt-robed guards dead or leaving.

And the pyres at the street corner
added to page by page
smoldering among the righteous.

The secrets coded, the hillside with its kings
stares down at us, the undecipherable,
the tablet that means victory. Whose? When?
The clay messages wash down to pebble
the scroll torn, packing for urns
    fair face   *engrained*
is all it tells us.

Water, fire, enemy bombardment
the careless sky, the slow damp of nightfall
the gathering and division
Khufu, Thebes, Alexandria
Rome, Monte Cassino.

Leather reeks an invitation.
I sit by the wall
of a deep well
while the slow fire of hours
darkens the pages.

PROPHET

In the fifteenth year of the emperor Tiberius
he hunted hives of wild bees
breaking open the hollows of wood or bone
seizing the sweet marrow.
Quicker than grasshoppers
he crunched wing and belly.
His face gnarled under the sun.
At night he crawled under
a goatskin. The air was thin out there
the stars big as melons.
The brook for water or washing in
or to cleanse an occasional stranger of his wickedness.
His hair matted. His dry beard
bristled away from his jaw.
Ravens flew by sometimes. Small groups of men
he shouted to, came, bringing others.
Clearly the world couldn't go on like this.

THE FOUR HORSEMEN

In our country the hills lie like tawny lions
green in spring, turning yellow with summer
here and there oak trees, with cattle under them
and in the broadest valleys, villages.

If strangers come along, we notice them.
Like those four, resting their horses
by the small stream there, under the oak tree.

Riders, and even from the distance
I can tell their horses are splendid, well-fed
faster than ours, and their trappings expensive.

Even from here they seem unusual travelers.
There's the one with the sorrel, a heavy man
black-bearded, restless, he aims his gun
at every bird, as if eager for hunting.

The thin one can't stand still either.
He is picking the stalks that grow around him
stripping the oats off, twisting the hollow stems
into knots and whistles. His horse is the black stallion.

And the plump palomino, stomping to be off
belongs to the man in the pale overcoat
who remains stock still, as if content where they are.

The fourth, in the yellow Stetson, waits apart from the others.
Whether he is their friend or enemy is hard to say.
Have they come for a duel in this deserted pasture?

I would go close if I dared, either to welcome them
to the village or find out their business.
But there is something so strange in their manner—

the oats falling back in a circle around them, the ground
growing dark, a cloud breaking the sun's warmth.
Better go back to town and see what's doing.

Those four may mean no harm, but no good certainly.
And I keep thinking of the balance of things
and how we might change should they settle among us.

MR. D

I think of you sometimes, how you came.
You were in brown, a patterned garment,
putting your hand on my forehead—yes
it was hot—and my tongue

was loose in my mouth, my eyes rattled
in sockets grown too large. Each part
of myself departed from every other.
I was a grand central station of departures

a kind of wormy seedbed, like your coat
a patchwork. Baling wire was what I needed
to keep the straws of me all together.
I didn't care much. And you were gentle.

You softened the pillow where my head sank
into a swamp. You helped me settle
my parts on the raft I was floating off on.
I slept easy knowing you were there.

You told me how to dream without dreaming
like the roots under the snow in winter.
Dark, and knowing that darkness, warm
and held like a comfort around me.

LANGUAGE

These are the times when I want to speak with you,
when my own thoughts are echoes. Look at the child, all
in proportion, or tell me the name of this flower—
questions and exclamations, nothing unusual
nothing I could not say as well to another

But my question is now how can you hear
me, not under the earth that I stamp on,
sprinkle with flowers, you are nowhere

not the bird pecking across this June
or the insects racking forth at dusk
complaints and melodies, they do not reach you
not in the fog or sun, high up in the ether,
only in this one grey circle, this on-
ly that still keeps you, clutches you here, and asks.

My eyes grew wide. Like a mole out of light
I could see the damp wall of my cage. The sun
was my desire. But I rejoiced that under
the earth in this bare place, the sound
of my prayers echoed. They sprang straight above.
I thanked God for the life of his creatures.

And in that dark I was in the company of creatures
greater than man. One led me to the light.
I had longed to see it in the world above
to look once again on the whole sun
a blaze so enormous it came as a sound
nearly unbearable breaking into my dungeon there under.

And with the creatures of day I entered the sun
whose light shines out through all things of the upper world.
    Its sound
the canticles of all above rooted in that praise deep under.

ON MUSIC

An Ode in the Baroque Manner
For Music by Purcell
To the Memory of R.S.

1

Let music which first set the skies in place
And made the earth through heavenly harmony
And round it sent the spheres circling in space
Subject to laws that lent to all things grace
        And motion—as the sea
        The wind, the atoms stirred
    Into perfection by music's melody—

Let music mourn her passing from this sphere
To that high morning. Let our notes declare
The spirit present that still must loiter here.
As waves from the pool's center wear
The startled shape after the center's gone
As notes still linger after the stricken keys.

2

As water over water lifts and wells
Layer on layer from weed-forested
Canyons of ocean's floor, up onto shelves
Of blue-green tropics, striking earth's shores. And led
Yet upward, waves of motion still ascend
Above earth's edge, above the looms and mines
        Quarries of stone and sand
        Whence grow by artful hands
        The monuments of land—

So over all that the earth refines
And changes, go the waves of air
High into noon to build cathedrals there
Where music's hands like skilful carpenters
Set out the buttress, shape the nave, beam over
All heaven with roofs of crystal melody.
Towers of sound the ears make visible!

Hear music's mighty structure as it grows
Before the last notes fall
Hear music rising that can outlast all.

3

Hear music rising that all loss repairs,
Age after age the monuments of air
Appear once more, old patterns ever new
In fresh and polished hue
As clear as at the first creation laid.
First Form that still all other forms contains
Repeated as the music soars again!

4

Let music, which out of jarring elements,
Chaotic atoms, first brought harmony
With God's hand guiding, carved out fire from night
Water from air and the earth from sea,
Renew us now as once more notes create
The heart's strong fortress, set on high
Radiant for an hour over us
To fall again after the last notes die.

Eternally new, yet old
Ever the same, like gold
Beat to new forms, like wind

Tuning the shaken air
Shifting the hearers' blood.

Players and listeners change
And instruments and air
Yet the same motion shimmers there
Making the world again through music's might
Constructed, like the heavens, of air and waves and light.

THREE

THE WOMEN OF PERSEUS

DANAE

1

I am caught here
in the held air
while outside the day
moves in the leaves.

Voices ripple
from far away,
the road disappears
in the dusty wind.

My blood sounds in my ears
like a river of brass
and the hills at the sky line
turn bronze with blossoms.

My thoughts wither
and vanish in circles where I imagine
down by the stream the footpath
crowded with passers.

Unreal from this distance
the processions as on a vase
the lovers leaning on one another
the world going about its business.

And my life here
an echoing bell
calling me nowhere,
the days rising and falling like wheatfields.

2

Night is my own.
The tower a shadow in shadows.
Down its sides run
ladders of leaves

shining vines and tendrils
stairways of broken mirrors
the rivers flash by
dreaming.

And the fish in their shifting schools
catch the light
like a secret.

Birds drowse in the trees
and the light lies over the white fields,
all taut, sheer surfaces,
that resound for a moment
the echo of light.

3

The days go by in gold
lazy and bright
warm in reflection
where waves shallow up yellow sands.

I catch light in my arms.
Dust powders the air
and the motes
spatter its rays in blinding echoes.

Soft as the chaff
that drifts from the winnowed grain
the sun heaps down on me
covers me in drifts

and the warm waves harden
into sinews of bronze.
Radiant with sun
my lover presses upon me.

4

First my father set me in this tower
among tripods burning with incense,
pampered with waiting women, fed on dishes of gold,
my garments bordered in purple, my arms
circled by amulets rich with jewels.

My handmaidens laugh, weaving endless garlands of flowers
and green.
The tower is fragrant and airy, and I can see far into distance.

I would rather live in a cottage by the rough waves,
the wife of a fisherman, waiting at evening for the day's
small catch
or in the hut of a ploughman in a stone-blunted upland.

The old man my father most of all fears time,
the grey already creeps in his beard and his hair,
jealous that his child grows beautiful beside him,
fears his own seed, knowing he will go down,
his strength stolen nightly, rising in his children.

I have lain with the sun, my lover,
and the sun's child will burst forth from my dark
at morning.

5

It is dark as the underworld here and when I try
to lift my head I strike the rough top
of the chest that they put me in. I still hear echoes of blows
on the top hammering home, splinters torture my fingers
where I struggled against the wood. I cannot see
to ease them out. My head aches from striking
the lid of the chest. I cannot raise my knees.
I screamed but heard no one. They worked in silence.

Now beaten by waves the box lurches and turns
rolling me here and there. The holes left for air
take in water. Already it sloshes
around me. I am cold, and the child with me
cries. The air reeks of him. He searches
with puny hands for my breast. His mouth
blind in the dark plucks at me. I am thirsty.
My father had been kinder to kill me outright
with a clean stroke. I am sick
with tossing. The box closes in, the water rises.
They have left me no means to destroy myself.

Starve, drown, suffocate.
These are my gifts
from my father who starved me of love
from my lover who drowned me in love
from my son for whose birth I die in this stinking box.

Zeus, who descended in sunlight
if once I shone in your favor
when your bright form grew in sudden rays
remember your son.

6

Now I live in the fisherman's cottage I once longed for.
The sea snarls over rocks, my son goes out with the fishers
or runs with the herdsmen's sons.
I wear the brown dress of the poor.

There is always something to do.
Water must be brought from the well
goats must be milked, cheese made, figs picked and dried,
olives pressed, and the eternal spinning.

The island is small and poor
the king's palace a house like the others.
Goats graze right up to the doorposts.
His brother is a fisherman.

They have given me a clumsy girl as a serving-maid
and the king looks my way too often.
The beauty that brought a god from heaven
withers in this forsaken island.

THE GRAEAE

We were always old, always turning away
from ripeness, without ever knowing springtime,
our hair hung in wrinkled strands
and no one ever looked at us.

We were born on a coast covered with grey clouds
all day. We have been here forever.
Grey sedge, grey rocks stretched up from dirty sand
a beach littered with weed and cast up timbers.

Nothing ever prospered here, the bushes covered with spines
a few water birds lost and quickly leaving
or adding a flat carcass to the draggled strand.
We had few hopes and nothing came of any.

Bit by bit we lost what little we had—
our teeth, our eyes, the rhythm of walking.
From the beginning the flat shore closed us in.
Three cold grey stones we sit here doing nothing.

MEDUSA

1

Had I but known when I saw the god approaching!
His horses pulled him briskly over the water
as on dry land, wreathed in seaweed, dripping,
his chariot shone gold in the warm summer.
I stood as he walked—the old man—up from the shore.
He climbed the temple stairs. He praised my grace.
I had never seen a god before.
He seized and raped me before Athena's altar.

It is no great thing to a god. For me it was anger—
no consent on my part, no wooing, all harsh
rough as a field hand. I didn't like it.
My hair coiled in fury; my mind held hate alone.
I thought of revenge, began to live on it.
My hair turned to serpents, my eyes saw the world in stone.

2

Whatever I looked at became wasteland.
The olive trees on the hill as I walked down
rattled in wind, then stood—as if a hand
had fashioned them of bronze. I saw the town
where I was raised become a stone. The boys
ran by as on a frieze, the charioteer
whipping his horses, held his arm, mid-air.

His horses stopped in stride. My hair
started to hiss. I hurried to my door.
The servant with his water jar upraised
stands there forever. I strode across the floor.
My furious glance destroyed all live things there.
I was alone. I am alone. My ways
divide me from the world, imprison me in a stare.

3

The prisoner of myself, I long to lose
the serpent hair, the baleful eyes, the face
twisted by fury that I did not choose.
I'd like to wake up in another place,
look for my self again, but there recur
thoughts of the god and his misdeed always—
the iron arm, the fall, the marble floor
the stinking breath, the sweaty weight, the pain,
the quickening thrust.

                  And now the start,
the rude circling blood-tide not my own
that squirms and writhes, steals from me bone by bone—
his monster seed growing beneath my heart,
prisoned within my prison, left alone,
despised, uncalled for, turning my blood to stone.

ANDROMEDA

I am terrified
marooned on a rock with a gale
freshening and the waves already
spatter me with spindrift.

What could my father be thinking of!
Listening to a two-faced oracle,
chaining me like a dog in this gnashing water.
It is low tide now—high tide will be the end of me.

I will either drown struggling against water
or be caught here by the monster from the sea
the claws searing me along the bone
the teeth quick cutting through flesh and nerve.

It is grim being a sacrifice.
The garlands, the watching crowds, cannot make me heroic.
My legs tremble and fire streaks across my brain
The roots of my hair are daggers.

If this were a story there would be a hero
to swim through the impossible waves, a sword at his belt.
He would cast off my chains, kill the monster, take me
out of this country mad with fear and riddles.

But all I am sure of is the explosion of waves,
my mother crying from the shore, the seething wings
of a large invisible bird circling the rock,
and the head of the monster coming up over the horizon.

PERSEUS

Because my mother mated with a god
I am by birthright a hero.
This brings responsibility. I have had to excel at games—
running, wrestling, throwing the spear and the discus,
and to undertake long journeys at a moment's notice.

My mother, being alone, brought me up as best she could
and I have always deferred to her wishes.
I have had to keep her unwanted lover at bay
and, as he was king, conciliate him too.
That is how I encountered my first adventure.

Bring back the head of Medusa, he told me
as if it were easy. Being young, I agreed.
I didn't even know where to find her, but I had help
from my brothers and sisters, the eternal gods.

They equipped me with wings, a shield, a sickle, and a cap
    of darkness
and pointed west. I flew up, high over the island
and saw how small it was. I flew on over the sea
until toward sunset I found the three old women.

They sat there, hardly moving, toothless and blind—
at least only one tooth and one eye among them,
which they passed round. I felt sorry for them
but I took the eye and the tooth anyway
and they pointed out Medusa.

She was asleep. Maybe she had once been beautiful
but no longer. Her face froze everyone to stone
but with my mirror-shield, cap, and sickle I could deal with her.
When I cut off her head, blood spurted in a fountain.
I had to wash myself in the sea. I had never killed anyone.

I put her head in the bag as I had been told to do
and started home. But I liked flying
and I turned south over Africa.
The desert looked endless—a few palm trees here and there
and towns where there were lakes or rivers.

The worst of it was the bag. Blood kept dripping out of it
and the serpent hair kept writhing.
Several times I almost threw it away.

As I neared Jaffa I saw a girl chained to a rock
the sea dashing over it. Her dark skin gleamed with water.
She wore jewels around her neck and nothing else.
Had she not been beautiful I might have gone on.
It was none of my business what she was doing there.

But then, sliding over the sea a monster appeared
her head twisting around, her body dipping
in and out of the waves. Steam came from her jaws
and scales dangled over her face like seaweed.
Clearly I was destined to do battle.

She was harder to kill than Medusa.
I had to keep flying around her,
invisible, yet in reach of the heavy tail
the spinning jaws. The sea grew bloodier
until at last she sank like a punctured kettle.

I married the maiden, freezing all objections

with the look on Medusa's face
and came home, spellbound the wicked lover,
made the fisherman king. He married my mother
and I became king in Argos.

Now I live idly here, Andromeda beside me
still beautiful, though slow in conversation,
asking myself, was I really a hero?
Or was it the weapons? Could anyone have done it?

After all, what is a kingdom?
The flying, the thrust of battle, the danger,
even the smell of blood, the writhing monsters—
dream or nightmare, then I truly lived.
And was that all? There must be more than this.

FOUR

AFTER SEPTEMBER

Autumn breaks over you
the clean wind
sweeps under the door
opens the sky.

Fruit rolls out of grocers' bins
grapes, cheap now
apples—juice flies out of them.

Red fires in the toyon
they tumble down hill
among walnuts' yellow
mixed everywhere.

Never such air as this.

You'll be looking for love
if you haven't yet found it.

LOVE SONG

Old Owl is gone.
No hoot from him in a fortnight
and the mice in the bush are saying their prayers:
    Let Old Owl be gone for a long time
    May he never come back!
    May some bigger bird in the sky
    Peck out those living eyes
    And clean him down to the last feather
    Till they blow away in the wind.
    May a great Mouse somewhere under the moon
    Pounce on him
    Shred him to a shriveled string.

And the small birds shrill louder than ever:
    Morning is here and Owl is gone!

Mockingbird, King of Day, leaps up
on his telephone pole
cartwheels in air
comes home precisely
not missing a note:
    Morning has come and Great Owl is gone.

Come soon, sweet Owl.
I miss your velvet note
and the soft slip of your wing.

INTO THE BESTIARY

1   THE OWL INSIDE

I hide my eyes in my hands
and he glares at me
red eyes make pools in my darkness
his beak yellow
smooth between my fingers
the left eye looks in my right
round and capable
the right squints after mice in the hollow
behind the eyes
behind the owl
are the creatures of that forest
a spotted moth
flaps past
a jaguar's tail
whisks out of sight
a whale's white teeth
an embryo
the sea urchin becomes aster becomes centipede
clouds pass   the forest darkens
green algae spread in lines over swamp water
grids on a map   the explosion
of a green rocket
oysters   birdwings   islands
in the owl's world nothing is equal.

2   THE BIRD LAGOON

Eleven swans ride these murky passages
as to a wedding on the Thames
their white plumes stretching.
A black-billed mother chides her ducklings;
back they go, red heads dipping under shrubbery
at the pool's edge. Flamingos
stand in the shallows by mud towers.
Each guards a single egg.
And the customers
drop paper cups into the lagoon.

Round about, round about
they bob, with the cruise boats, the strollers
the macaws and ibises, the
wounded eagles, and the high lonely white
black-headed vulture who contemplates
the fragile structure of his paradise.

3 THE FISH CAGE

The amateur astronomer
has tipped his telescope downward
underwater
and the minnows become planets
around the great octopus, the sun

which is reflected, this being
night, in the eye
of a giant manta ray
that slips like a cloud
among nebulae of mackerel.

The constellations heave and form again
like chorus girls.
His notebooks are voluminous
he cannot keep track of the changes
in this unplotted sky.

He calls for the constancy of Arcturus
of Mizar, Alioth, Polaris
the Dioscuri, Pleiades, the Centaur
but finds only meteors, falling stars
comets, nothing spectacular
as the pure spark of Hesperus at evening.

Despairing, he throws down the telescope
turns archeologist. Certainly those old bones,
he cries, will lie steady among the shards
dead pottery, downed columns, they will stay there
not moving till I come to them.

4   THE MOLE RIDE

Under the paw of the glass mole
(opaque, the sun shines through)
the lines in the sky are pink
where the blood runs in its web
like an early peach in blossom.

Under the giant paw—or shrunk
to mole dimension—I wait
to be dragged by the blind
inquisitive muzzle into the dark
house of the mole,
a rag doll,
his plaything.

The glass eye of the mole opens,
sees nothing.
I labor through those labyrinths
where secret entrances.
hide under the loose earth,
to be at ride's end rocketed
into the strange blink of day.

DESPITE ALL THAT

she is still telling the tides where to begin.
Under her circle the blood of the lunatic
rises. She calls to the man with the knife.
The hot housewife slides out of the scraps
of the kitchen to the lover under her shadow.
And the seed-burst herring listen for her coming
in the long lurching of the sea.

Water drips from her into the veins of cabbages
and corn silk, and vines send loose tendrils
high toward her crossing. Neither the sunflower
nor day's-eye finds gods more loving
than this enchantress who changes nightly
casting her monthlong circle of chains
over the losers.

WATCHING THE BREAK-UP

1

Trying to feel sure when you are not sure
is like walking in quicksand, though I never
saw any, or even walked in a swamp
except in the everglades, where paths are everywhere
made of boards. An alligator was
in a pool where fish swam by his mouth
ready for eating, not seeming to care about that.
I met a man who shot 12 crocodiles
one morning on safari. These tears are not
crocodile tears, though I have never seen
a crocodile cry.

2

The clock is a chatterbox, always buzzing about your ear
going rat-a-tat-tat. Bad as a fly.
But you can't swat it. It has to wake you up
at 6 o'clock. Still that's not fair
to the clock, hardworking night and day
like your heart. Both telling your time,
telling your time.
I know of no things less dispensable
than clocks and hearts
even though they break wide open at 6 a.m.
with their alarm.

3

Be undisturbed—you heard only half the story.
But be compassionate—do whatever you can do.
And learn to swim if you live near the ocean.
Many have drowned even in tiny rivers.

DRIVING EASTWARD

we enter the City of Morley's Ridge
the roads guarded by radar
and the dog sniffing the curb hollers
don't speed.

The horizon just tickles the sun's edge
the elms meander down Main Street
and a rooster wakes up behind Mullens' Bar.

The Coffee Shop wedged between Hotel
and Dry Goods blinks with one eye
Closed one door says, but the other says Open.

We'll never know now. And the heat wriggles
out of the big hay field on the corner
north of 10th and Main. We smell the sweet

hot scent of ragweed, watch a bird
flash off the wire toward that grove of cottonwoods
as the town settles for day behind Morley's ridge.

DOWN, DOWN

I am says the bulldozer
singing brighter than the birds
a thousand birds on a thousand branches
sing no merrier than I

and the crickets' *alas*
the brittle scraping
of a million legs together
or the bellowing of frogs.

I am and send my weighty message
over the hills at daybreak
breaking hills
I am stronger than the mountain.

I push up the knotted roots of sycamores
a hundred summers gathering.
I shake the sunflowers
where the spotted eggs are hiding.

I stamp down this terrace. I descend
to the Pleistocene. This was a lake
then rock. I make it a meadow.
No ages for me. An afternoon is enough.

I am says the bulldozer
and compassed round with music.

UNWINDING THE GLACIER

Not for one moment does this scowler stop
cleaning the monster slope, packing its load
of windowless cathedrals, hulking ships,
untidy monuments.

What trees one winter
went down under snow, pack ice burns steadily
across the striae of a widow mountain.
Summer carves its skin with sweat.

Massive and slow we ride these cold windings,
building our Roman road and aqueduct,
riding the rails that stagger as we pass.
Out of its melting pours the clear water—green, pure,
the halo of saints, presenting the piedmont
with its vines and grains—substance of sacrament.

IN SUMMER

It comes in summer
In our tree it sings
It rides our bones

It cries Everything
Grows but to shatter
It speaks of roses

Waves broken, the ring
Of lapsing water
The slip of stones

In streams, down hillsides
Emptiness it says
All wasted, gone.

So it in summer sings.
The holly white with bloom.
No thing its lie believes.

FIVE

It was a war that nobody won. Both sides were held in balance, each move checked before it was made, by the brilliant espionage of Count Hugo von S. and the Baroness de B., representing our C.E. countries on the one hand and that of an obscure but dogged agent, whose name has not come to light, on the other. Though he seemed inept, often being glimpsed by the C.E. agents outside their various headquarters, he must have had a superior operation behind him, for our people were never able to shake him off despite constant movement. Unprepossessing, forever merging with the background, even the power(s) he worked for not yet ascertained—

EXCERPT FROM *The Memoirs of Marie Hessenburg-Rothe*, tr. M.K. SHELDON.

IN MEDITERRANEAN AIR

AT THE VILLA

Who listens to us? Out past the terrace the spy
hides behind Venus's statue
moving nearer, his cheek flat
mottled with rotting marble.
The ebon-eyed goddess
turns black with night.

And the footsteps rustle closer
in a dirty wind that casts over us
grit and a film of leaves. The garden
laid down under heat. The fountains'
statues cracked in sun. Is he still
flat to Venus's buttocks or is he

wrestling with Adonis by the garden path?
They should have been left together
those two. Let us look at the map now
spread out under the thin torch.
It will draw him, the cheating moth,
antennae spread. His instructions

crackle in the air, signal storm
to some of us. A storm would cool us all
take the sand from the insufferable air, restore
the long look between the statues
down to the gone garden's end, put him in his
     trenchcoat
drenched anyhow, lurking out there unsheltered.

THE PURSUER

He might come through any door—
the thick oak at the top of the curving stair
the painted panels leading to the study
the knobbed iron from the driveway, with its
    broken lock,
or the French windows opening on the terrace.
Even, God forbid, from the plain door in the passage
leading down dark stone steps to the cellar.

And I, standing in the massive marble hall,
a piece on a chessboard
moving from the square of pale Perlato
to the dark veins of Turquesa.

Those quarries make the whole house cold
with their ungiving surfaces. And the room so bright
it is like a stage, the audience hidden
in the shifty vines of the terrace
or the shadow above the balcony.

For all I know the walls papered with nymphs and
    fountains
and flowering trees are peopled with watching eyes
and the Venetian mirrors counterfeit.

I pretend to be looking at the statues,
copies of ancient art—Actaeon, Artemis,
Laocoon wreathed in serpents—

while I search for a faint heelmark,
a spot of water, a speck of lint, a shred of paper.

But I find no clue, and logic cannot help me
nor the strained sensing for the hidden breath
the scent of oleander crushed, the faint electric aura
of the body. I must go at once

lock myself incommunicado in the study
take the broad circling stairway into shadow
or the iron doorway leading to the forest.
I have to choose. I could meet him anywhere.

IN THE GARDEN

Sun or rain I am out here, shoes overflowing,
or holding to a slice of shadow, while the heat
cracks the ground all around me.
Sweat glues my skin, or else wind
carves my face with granules.

They sit inside with their tea or stroll
after dark on the terrace. There's little shelter,
they have seen to that. If they talk
they find an upstairs room—there's only rotten vines
   to cling to;
the stones crumble under my toes. I'm no acrobat.

They think they'll outlast me. But they don't dare
leave in the shined Mercedes, ready in the driveway
lest I find the map in the cupboard, the code
under the faded icon in the passage.
They bore one another. The cook never washes his hands.

They'll crack before I do. The khamsin is about to begin—
fifty days of swirling sand. They'll be trapped for sure
with the dirty cook and the rough butler
who shadows them. And I, like a sundial,
patient, enduring, forgiving, in the garden.

THE CHASE

Sooner or later we must go after them.
Clumsy fools, they can never slip away
without stumbling into a table in the corridor
crashing the lamp. They bring the whole house down
every door opens, lights go on, the butler comes up from
the wine cellar.

They make a run for it; the car in the driveway is locked
the battery dead, but they get it rolling
and we follow over roaring bridges, through broken
hedgerows,
turning like wind-devils. Smash over the guardrail.
Their car spirals. They melt into the forest.

We are on foot now, stalking the pine trees
and it's beginning to snow. My hand aches
where the bullet grazed the little finger.
Ice stiffens my town shoes. I am lost.
They have got away once more undeserving.

ON THE TRAIN

Forget day and night; this is all you can think of.
Forget sleep, breakfast, keeping appointments.
You eat when you can, doze under a tarpaulin,
on trains, in the back seats of rented cars.

Your mind stays on the treadmill.
What it is you are after. You are not even sure,
but it is there somewhere. You have to find it.
That couple ahead—the man with the blue glass eye

the woman in the modish hat, they have hidden it.
The train lurches on. You must rifle the luggage.
What good if they sleep? You wouldn't dare touch them.
You need accomplices, and you haven't any.

You are alone with the search and not much time.
Something must turn your way, you can't trail them forever.
Her gloved hand gestures and you strain to hear.
The glass eye follows you like a periscope.

INCOGNITO

Do they know I have been in the villa?
That I am the mouse that snoops in the corridor
midnight to morning, hearing them joust in bed?
I am the limping man who brings the firewood
my wool cap low on my forehead, my beard gone wild.
I am the plump girl who sells them vegetables;
my head touches the cook's as we lean over the basket.
I was the wisecracking messenger with wilted roses,
the man with the telegram. I carried your bags
when you took the through train to the south.
I was the old gentleman with the cane two seats behind you.
You are such blunderers. Yet you keep it hidden,
what I am after, however I hide myself.

HEADQUARTERS

The radio's gone off. I've set the band
at the right time and the number, and nothing comes of it.
A crackle sometimes; it's still alive.
I'm where I should be. The world's disappeared out there.

Why don't they signal? Have they forgotten me?
I tried the telephone, but it kept ringing.
Something's gone wrong.

I can't give up when I am so close to it,
watching the lichens grow on the statues,
sheltering behind them in the sirocco.

I'm the cat that walks at night
sleeps with one eye. I'm a tree. I'm a statue.
I'll get at the secret, though there's no one to take it to.

THREE

God, how I envy them! Always together.
The train sways past villages, the dining car
sparkles. They whisper together.
The wine drips amber into their glasses.
He touches her hand in a careless movement,
puts a cigarette in a slim holder,
lights it, passes it to her. They play this game
over and over. It is all for me.

I sit behind the newspaper at the next table—
France-Soir. "Liebling," he says, "liebling,
souviens-toi, l'été dernier sur la plage..."
No one else cares. The waiter a smiling simpleton.

I was careful at the last station.
I boarded without a glance at them.
They know, they know, teasing the scattered table crumbs.
They look for me, watching them, wait for me everywhere.

OUTSIDE

Last night the birds outside had their feathers ruffed all right!
Cold as six pigeons! Beer froze on pantry shelves.
Do they know how I feel out here alone?
What if I went away? Who'd care for their pas de deux.
It's only for me
they bolt the iron-studded door at night
pull the rotten drapes near the terrace
and embrace under the lamps by the upstairs window.

It's like marriage. What a waste if I left them!
They pretend to hide messages while I am watching,
or half-burn a paper, throw the rest in the fireplace;
they laugh while I sift their ashes
for a scrap of *Die Zeitung* faintly underlined.
They are my life. I love them. They hate one another.

THE PARTY

I've stayed out here so long my head is ablaze with blossoms.
Stems are growing up all around me bumpy with buds.
It's springtime. My short-wave sputters birdsongs.
The owls whoop all night like lusty nightingales.

The villa is all lit up. Tables swim in flowers—
peonies, ranunculus. I can't keep up with the guests,
generals in full regalia. Bosoms curve under diamonds,
the chandeliers shine, crystal hides the table,
notes pass from hand to hand with the champagne.

Perfume seeps from the terrace in waves
I am about to drown in it! It's been so long!
I'd like to run in, my dusty shoes on the carpet,
snatching up wine, crying *Salut*, and embrace every one of them.

THE DESIGN

In what design am I, here in the garden—
the garden with its diamond paths
that criss-cross behind hedges,
the flowers settled in their chosen plots
divided by size, function, color even,
the flowers adjusted to conditions:
sun, the minerals of the soil, the frequency of rain—
none deviate, weeds are removed,
all rejuvenate, fertilizing one another
with their special insects—not only bees
but flies, wasps,
even wind. I alone. My function
is merely to watch and wait.

How do I fit in? If I move my foot
I trample on hyacinth, perfume of broken stems,
the petals wetting my boot soles, slippery, yellow.
Pollen lies broken open on the dark green of the stems.
Hostile my foot on the ground, pressing in gentle violence
across the grass. Why am I here?
I am curious. But to break
even the flowers in springtime
argues force, overturning, behavior
I should hate to own.

What is the difference between them and me?
We are for beauty, harmony, joy, utopia

here among the hyacinths, the bells' bloody coral,
the yellow cries of the pistils for rape,
for birdwings, the visits of flying hordes.
Nothing lies between us
but lawns and the cold statues
rotting by the old walls.

I have imagined a paradise where no serpent enters
without apples hidden under
the cushions of the parlor, or under
the marble set at tangents in the gallery.
Yet we stand here on both sides of the wall
listening to one another. Our inner states
of love, happiness—it is a strain to bear all this.
Happiness itself is a terror.
I can only conclude with the secret:
if is the wall of thorns; it is the fruit in the parlor;
it is the flight and the chase; it is the disillusion;
it is what we are all afraid of.

SIX

EXILES

We can never go home now.
What there was is cut down—
trees, house wall, under the tractor
woods we ran in at night, twisted
up, the roots startled with earth
shreds clotted around them.

But we have beat them to the next station,
some of us, and enough trees for fires,
houses, whatever we make of them.
We brought what we could carry.
Enough maybe when we learn
what grows wild here, what we can count on.

We sort out noises at night
watch where we walk by day.
But the sky lurks like a spy. Our words
turn against us, what we keep is a threat.
They're bound to be after us.

CROSSING

The end of it came sudden.
The brakes locked and we skidded
half the tires blacked the road
the back end skewed
came round
and we went spinning over the edge.

We shouted at the black water
where the river slammed up to meet us.
Then the great smash and we
breathed deep while the black stuff
moved in, mixture of mud, sewage, debris,
banging against something   slowed   stopped.

All close as a mine
and no lamp,   the fluid embracing us,
and caught in the torn shred of air
conjuring up torches, divers
and the scum-lit direction of morning.

THE MESSAGE

Who who—the owl
called through the black. Soft
were his words. The answer
soft. I heard

through black sleep. Not to wake
while owls rummage the trees
search runnels of grass, not seen,
heard, heard into dream.

There was a man unseen
before, shone on the porch of dream
the light behind him bright
his face seen and never seen

before. Clear I saw him
and what he said true, while
the owl searched. I forgot
his words that told so much.

AFTER EXILE

It was not the dream that did it.
It only reflected
the serpent of power rising
from the roots of earth
into the head where the hair
flew out like sprays of a flowering tree.
Blossoms falling wherever the feet
half-touched the ground
the girl with new-risen breasts
running through doorways
into the green garden
where trees grew overnight
placing themselves in trim rows
and the blooms of azaleas, acacia,
and pomegranate split the air with color,
whole skies of blooms covered the ground
but it was the fountain that rose like a serpent
ricocheted over every tendril of the green garden.

THE TURN

Like lying down for winter, all life
drained—mud at the base of a pool—
scum freezing over—the bones bent like ribbons
around the limp center
the saints locked in their chambers
saying I am nothing.

Morning not a clatter of bird notes and wings
but a sour taste and voices,
no reasons to go or stay, only to keep the sky
and earth apart. Caught in the knuckled hand
a fistful of clay.

This is when it turns, begins to shoot
up the green brace that breaks open the hand
and suddenly into the white light
of ordinary morning like a reed
or a vine or a tree that will scratch at heaven.

LISTENING TO COLOR

Now that blue has had its say
has told its winds, wall, sick
sky even, I can listen to white

sweet poison flowers   hedge autumn
under a sky white at the edges
like faded paper. My message keeps

turning to yellow where few leaves
set up first fires over branches
tips of flames only, nothing here finished yet.